NOMADS WITH SAMSONITE

NOMADS WITH SAMSONITE

Timothy Bradford

BlazeVOX [books]

Buffalo, New York

Book design by Geoffrey Gatza
Cover art: *Excerpt (suprematist evasion)* by Julie Mehretu
Courtesy of the artist and Marian Goodman Gallery, Private Collection

First Edition
ISBN: 978-1-60964-045-3
Library of Congress Control Number: 2010939079

BlazeVOX [books]
76 Inwood Place
Buffalo, NY 14209

Editor@blazevox.org

publisher of weird little books

BlazeVOX [books]

blazevox.org

2   4   6   8   0   9   7   5   3   1

BlazeVOX

Acknowledgements

My gratitude to the publishers, editors, and readers of the following journals in which poems from this manuscript, sometimes in different forms, originally appeared:

42opus, Bombay Gin, CrossConnect, DIAGRAM, Drunken Boat, Eclectica, ecopoetics, H_NGM_N, The Melic Review, Mudlark, No Tell Motel, Poems & Plays, Redactions, Runes: A Review of Poetry, Softblow, Terminus, and *Upstairs at Duroc*

"Ophelia's Dream" was one of a group of three poems that received a 2007 Dorothy Sargent Rosenberg Poetry Prize and appeared on the prize's website; "My Secret Fantasy Life" was included in the anthology *The Bedside Guide to No Tell Motel – Second Floor*; "The Poet at Seventeen" was included in the anthology *Ain't Nobody That Can Sing Like Me: New Oklahoma Writing*

A heartfelt thanks to the following teachers, mentors, colleagues, and friends, who influenced and/or improved these poems in myriad ways: Ann Savage/East (in memoriam), Betty Shipley (in memoriam), Ai (in memoriam), Karen Holt, Carol Hamilton, Carol Koss, Stephen Garrison, Daniel Vilmure, Ann Neelon, Carolyne Wright, Anne Waldman, Anselm Hollo, Andrew Schelling, Julie Patton, Kevin Killian, Ali Zarin, Jonathan Skinner, Lisa Lewis, Alfred Corn, Toni Graham, E. P. Walkiewicz, Linda Leavell, Mark Parsons, Tom Dvorske, Michelle Brown, Carmella Braniger, Monique Ferrell, Solomon Quaynor, Dinah Cox, Miriam Love, Constance Squires, Michael Mobley, and Kristine Ervin.

A special thanks to these generous human beings and talented writers/editors for their critical attention to the manuscript as a whole: Robin Bradford, Clay Matthews, Matt Hollrah, Jerry Williams, Nate Pritts, and Eleni Sikelianos. And to the latter three, my deep appreciation for their kind words on this collection.

Endless gratitude to Geoffrey Gatza for his enthusiasm for this book and for his tireless work on behalf of the *polis*.

Grosses bises to Julie Mehretu for the right to reproduce *Excerpt (suprematist evasion)* on the cover.

And to my parents, Peter and Georgann Bradford, thank you for this precious human birth and for endless encouragement.

For Tamara, Tristan, and Dimitri

Contents

4. The Comedy of Light

5. All Other Unities

We'd rather have the iceberg than the ship,
although it meant the end of travel.

—Elizabeth Bishop

1. THE LOVE KITCHEN

WHY DOGS INGEST ANYTHING WHILE THE HUMAN MOUTH REMAINS SO SENTIMENTAL

1.

Things I've seen dogs eat: dog food, squirrels, cats, grass,
side of a 1972 GMC truck, *Heart of Understanding* by
Thich Nhat Hahn, Scooby snacks, dirt, fast food (including
most of the bag), horse shit, cow shit, human shit,
other dogs, a bloated human corpse on the banks
of the River Ganges.

Twelve thousand years ago, in a site near Jerusalem, a man
was laid in a grave, right hand cradling a dog.

Who has not at least slept in the same room
as those with the most omnivorous mouths?

2.

My older son teaches my younger son to pray—
These are your eyes, and these are your arms,
and these are your ears, and these are your legs.

Part of a prayer said much earlier—
Wolf, don't eat my eyes, Wolf, don't eat my arms,
Dog, don't eat my legs, Dog, don't eat my nose.

Part of an antiphony to be mouthed later—
Sir, don't torch my ear, God, don't eat my eyes,
Work, don't eat my arms, Lady, not my legs.

I, being Buddhist, don't believe in prayer
to save *my* skin despite the shape I'm in—
eaten by my work clothes, eaten by my school clothes,
eaten by the horses who live in the yard,
eaten by the Maenads, eaten by my TV,
eaten by my own two sons who learn to pray.
And the gods in the yard and the woman at school
and the books on the shelf and the kitchen knife too.
Eaten, eaten, eaten, eaten, eaten, eaten, eaten up.

"Rimpoche, I warn you seriously. I have some medical knowledge;
your disciple may . . . be driven to madness by the terror
he experiences. He really appeared to feel himself being
eaten alive."

"No doubt he is, but he does not understand
that he himself is the eater."

3.

You be the dog and I'll be the catcher.
    No, *I'll* be the catcher and *you* be the dog.
The catcher.
    The dog.
The catcher.
    The dog. Remember, the catcher always gets it
    in the end.
The *dog* always gets it in the end.
    Well, the catcher first . . .
And the dog in the end.
    But first a surprise, a growl, bared teeth,
    a lunge to scratch or bite!
So you will be the dog?
    Maybe the dog and maybe the wolf.
    You won't know till you're in my teeth.
Not a chance. I'm too careful.
    The chase makes one careless.
No way, I'm too aware.
    The fur makes one awareless.
Careless, awareless, the dog always gets it
in the end.
    Not till the very last, very final, on-the-leash-
    and-wearing-muzzle very last end.

4.

Do we have such horrors inside our body?

Nothing was horrible about the beginning. My pack
flowed around me like dancers at a party.
The sun lulled in the trees, the dry
heat of the day not yet on. My bow was taut,
my step, light, as if all those years of hunting
either fell from me or buoyed me—I was
other than myself. Instinct led me
up an unknown slope to a miraculous grove

16

radiating like the sun itself. The moist sounds
of panting and licking died down as my hounds
fell in around me. We stepped nearly in time,
breathed the same rhythm, and from the edge
of the grove, I saw, in water like silver, her body
pulse perfect, a white heat mirage. Then I,
suddenly another hairier, swifter animal,
watched closely as my own sharp-toothed hounds
flayed the skin from my muscles, bared the miracle
of fasciae and nerve from inside my body
with their generous, ungentle mouths.
Seen for the first time, and for the last,
the network of optimism I was.

Middle Songs

Acrid odor from green pecan's fuselage

My youngest son collects them and deems

Good, bad, good, good

A man with one leg delivers a child
to the waiting bus

The __ank of _____ is missing
its *B*

Flint striking on the emptiness of all,
the fullness, and consciousness fuel

Hula forbidden here, no island

Sky a ring that holds us center, a friend
once suggested the clouds as mountains

Disbelief in this, what is   what is not

What is and is not, such as the baby changing
table in the restroom, which the Spanish
makes clear is not a place for changing babies
but merely their *pañals*

I'm alive like the metabolic potential of
Walmart-shopping middle America

I thrum like an emu

FIRST TREATISE

A car is a little miracle
that moves around.
You can sit inside
and be moved
by the car or move it,
if licensed. It is
a moving space. A house
moves much less but is
definitely a space
where you can store things
and live. Dead things
necessitate the opening
of the space to the outdoors, the biggest
of all spaces, where I sit now,
mind conjoined to sky
shot through with birds
and oxygen and the increasing
humidity from melting
snow, far from you and loving you
just the same, like a house
with all its windows open.

ANTHROPOLOGY OF LOVE

—from the spine of National Geographic, *October 2001*

You no longer mention light,
she wrote him from a Kansas rain forest
soon to be paved over for The China Tombs
Mall, complete with fountains like volcanoes,
display cases coddling Meave Leakey's
latest finds, and limited-motion dancing mechanical leopards.

He, a mollusk on the Swahili coast and spotted like a leopard,
wrote back to say ignoring light
is second nature to mollusks, akin to Richard Leakey's
ignorance of cloud formations, stingy rain forests
in the African sky. *We live by the heat of underwater volcanoes,*
unseen, and dream of being used as eternal cups inside China Tombs.

She read his reply, then stubbed her cigarettė out in the China Tombs
ashtray he'd bought her on their honeymoon when they loved like leopards,
ate fresh figs and oysters, toured the volcano.
Think of something bimorphic, like light,
the way it's a wave and particle. Or the rain forests
of Chile next to deserts. Or the Leakeys'

fondness for AC. You could return as a Leakey
hominid, but with flesh, and still play at mollusk in the China Tombs
Bar at night. I love you like a rain forest
breathes for the earth. Come back, my leopard.
She sent the request at first light
and wandered among small copper-pit slag-heap volcanoes

instead of working. At night, she burned like a volcano
while the mollusk traveled inland to help the Leakeys
look for fossils under sheer walls of light
west of Kenya's Lake Turkana, thousands of miles from the nearest China Tombs.
Unfortunately, everyone save Meave had been devoured by leopards.
Still, she sat looking, alone like an oasis rain forest.

"Meave," the mollusk called with a voice like charred rain forest,
"it's as hot as a fucking volcano
out here, not to mention all these pesky leopards.
Let's hitch back to Nairobi and use your Leakey
fame to score a hotel room with linoleum as cold as China Tombs.
Where Richard failed, I'll be as constant as the speed of light."

Weeks later, a final postcard reached her in Kansas, light through a rain forest
canopy. *Dear Sarah, Adieu. Didn't make the China Tombs but discovered the volcanic
love of Meave Leakey. Her paleoanthropologist kiss is pure leopard.*

MY SECRET FANTASY LIFE

Cassandra, the dental assistant,
welcomes me, is
real nice, makes me feel
right at home. She wears
scrubs, latex gloves, a blue paper mask,
and clear plastic eye protection.
She asks about
problem areas, and when she
has me down, my mouth
open wide and a large dental pick
scraping the grooves
on some sensitive tooth
in the back, she asks if I've
been to the state fair yet.

I nearly gag answering
with my tongue trying to lie down,
be polite, not follow her work
all over my mouth like a needy dog.
So I take to grunting. She
doesn't mind, responds
by asking more questions, increasing
the pressure and speed
of the dental pick until it begins
to nick at my gums
here and there. Behind
the oversized mirrored sunglasses
she's given me for protection,
I close my eyes and remember
that scene in *The Marathon Man.*
Cassandra could ruin my mouth
with a quick slip.
My leg twitches. I sweat.

And imagine her
astride me. She wears
her turquoise dental assistant's top,
nothing else, and rocks
gently back and forth,
like a chambered nautilus swims,

as she works.
Fear and eroticism are fine bedmates.
She stops asking questions, continues
with an intensity that feeds
my fantasy, makes the minute,
enormous pain almost bearable.

I want to open my eyes
and look at her, but when I do,
my fantasy goes askew. She's
at the wrong angle, has the wrong
grimace on her face, looks
like she could be scrubbing
the neck of some little kid in a tub,
determined beyond the kid or dirt or
tooth or husband or job that involves
looking into hundreds of mouths, all
with their own unique
mouth smells, weekly. So I
close my eyes again and try to imagine
the weight of her body
settling on me like an x-ray apron.

My fear? Vagina dentata? No, not teeth there. The teeth in our very own mouths. The
linguadental and labiodental sounds—*this fit, that fête, this fat, that fought, this foot*—
and their absence. The way we're born to gum, then chew, then, if we're lucky? gum
again. The singularly oracular symbolism of the mouth and the phantasms of worlds it
spews. Teeth in a kiss, or more so, a kiss without teeth. These little enamel plates of
clack-clack that fall out, hide under pillows, mutate into coins, scintillate in the sun,
work against the tongue, with the tongue, *by these teeth I thee wed*, the stain, the
decay, the loss. A weak spot in some god's plan, like knees. Or is it just our sin of
sugar? *Oh, little white sweets of sin, please stay firm in the sulci.*

Cassandra finishes. I am awake and sitting
upright, talking to the dentist.
She says, "Everything looks great," and I agree.
Sunlight, breaking through the clouds,
reveals a single bullet mark
in the window before us, but the surface
still has integrity, keeps
the animals out though they can
see us through the glass.

Bim Gets Breakfast in the Love Kitchen

—after a drawing by a child with autism

Bim gets breakfast, meaning
bread and butter, tea, and pork kidney
from Dlugacz's, or Lucky Charms.
Bim the faded foreground
of eyes' narrow aperture
focused on background.
His head a pale moon over
the constellation of the Love Kitchen's
multifarious bric-a-brac: picture
of a piggy bank, starry starry
wallpaper like the side of a Napoleonic
wrasse, flowers, candles, and a photo
of the sun. The window's frame above
shows the kitchen's walls to be
at least a foot thick, no brick
left unaccounted for, but three
vague dots make up the whole
of Bim's face above his Nehru jacket.
A constellation beyond words whirls
beside his small planet of a head
that contains so many
impressions of the universe's
constant flinging about of matter,
i.e., love, but lacks
a full mouth to voice them.

SEVEN-PART NOTE TO SUICIDE

1.

The suicides kept building, emboldened by the premise that anything asked for in the final note would be delivered—this reading from Mallarmé, that song in the !Kung tongue, a group of Nuer dancers, nearly naked, in the nave of the Unitarian church. Things finally reached a head when one suicide requested his body be brought to the alter and that, as the mourners filed by, they sample a small salty bit of him from his skull, opened in the back by the impact of a .44. The relatives and mourners balked, and the suicides calmed down, returned to their drawing boards and depressed lives.

2.

"I love you, you love me,
Soda pop, ice cream, 1, 2, 3,
Ho ho ho ho, he he he . . . "

      Blam.

3.

A white-columned New England-style church in Oklahoma imitates a white-columned neoclassical church in New England, which imitates a white-columned neoclassical church in England, which imitates a white-columned early Roman church, which imitates a white-columned Roman temple, derived from the Greeks. The suicides in all these imitations are different. There is no imitative suicide. Each dies by an original hand.

4.

Suicide, you've left this planet, where Jack Kerouac wrote, *We stopped in the unimaginable softness. It was as hot as the inside of a baker's oven on a June night in New Orleans. All up and down the street whole families were sitting around in the dark, chatting; occasional girls came by, but extremely young and only curious to see what we looked like* about Limón, Mexico. Suicide, have you ever been to Mexico? I've heard it's lovely there. Better than a loaded gun. Sweeter than arsenic in gin. Come away to Mexico with me, my sweet open-headed one, you pistol lover gone dim.

5.

If you've only thought of killing yourself, you don't understand this. If you've actually done it, suicide, I write this purely for you.

6.

It's getting late little back-of-head-lacking one. I tire and cannot comfort your bride, alive. I'm in the kitchen, head full of wassail, halfway between her antic storytelling grip on this world—keep talking and you're still alive—and you, silent, listening, eyes Chinese and death on your shoulder like a trained bird of prey. I beg off, return home, choose sleep and dream, not shuffle off.

7.

Suicide, it's 4:47 p.m., and the clear winter light is on the barren trees across the road. Suicide, my son is beautiful when I brush his teeth and see him. Suicide, staplers terrorize and argue your side of things, but tea is on my side and I win. Suicide, you loved the same book I do and never told me save via Morse code from the other side. Suicide, generous dollops of good oral sex and quality goaltending! Suicide, clean the dirt from your ears with fire, fir trees, water, and ether—I never knew you—suicide, this is a love letter, like the first you ever received: scented with cheap perfume, decorated with swirling hearts, folded into itself and promising warm grape lip gloss kisses on a cold winter day. Open it. Kiss me wholly.

TRANSLATION OF DISTANCE

They imagined days of vacation
via marks on the calendar, but in the actual
foothills of mental health
near Mt. Sanitas, so much muddier
than in memory, his mind goes
wrought iron fence. Among family,
some monks find sanity difficult.

His son disappears for a beat too long
—mountain lion?—then reappears
from the mouth of a plastic play castle
as a dog or feral cat,
as a boy with muddy knees.

The days pass like his wife's
family's slide show: scrambled images
click and whir into focus on the white wall.
Disembodied voices voice
captions from around
the darkened room. Sometimes
accord, sometimes not. Who will order
this inchoate history?

Later, on the porch, having forgotten
the *Vinaya Pitaka*'s prohibition of alcohol,
or pretending to some knowledge of the Vajrayana,
he relaxes with Drambuie and the words of Bodhidharma:

Open spaces—   *nothing holy.*

Relaxes is an anagram of *drunk, open* rhymes with *avoidance,*
and nothing can write the adequate weight
of mountain air pouring
over the pass from the west.
Over the bones of the day.

And the next day. And the next day,
he and his son find a memorial to
Chief Niwot, murdered with his people.
Later, at the town's public library, three

ripped Lakota-Sioux hand out books on child rearing
and hustle change.

During lunch in the library's café,
his son sees Boulder Creek as going up and up,
not spatially away. The monk reads
Basho's *Narrow Road to the Interior.*
His son climbs the creek to the sky.

Five miles. They walk five miles and eat and read.
A good day by most accounts. Now the moon
does not exist above the low, pregnant clouds.

He sheds his robes and becomes
an embryo inside
the illuminated house.

Lost Time for Rose

Let shiny black go with her belly
marked red in a field of broken
grave stones. Forgot to say, "I let
you go; tell your family—Theridiidae—
not to bite my family—XX, XY, XY—
ridge west of the North Canadian."

Out of the glass jar, her legs swarmed
like cilia in the lungs
to try on a mantle of fresh air.

I let her go, untamed. Some things beyond
domesticity. Like REM sleep.

Animals move through. Desecrated 8 mm
rewound and played again, with
stutters and gaps: a niece humming
jazz standards and I ride the mare,
dogs sicced on us by _____?,
and lizards witness with hidden eyes.
All strangely Celluloid, flat
on the screen of the mind rigged high
above the slumbering body.

My trainer's gone. I'm a lonely animal
on this swarming planet, with a den
of children, with visitors, but without
a trainer, the heart cannot see right.

Time to train me myself for the difficult
recognition of this family—this consciousness—
of light. Or time to run an advert: *Trainer
wanted, third stop from the sun.*

EDITION

And then only four days
left until
summer. Spring devoured

by the succulent cannas—
Bengal Tiger,
Minerva, and Miss Oklahoma.

Naked couples court on swings
in the dusk,
and Fragonard's painting too

hangs on the horizon as
large as a horse.
The days long

and desirable again. The miracle
of cucumber
and butter on bread at break time.

And no one threatens to bring
a pickax
down on his head, least of all

him. Gallant, all of us, as we witness
gas prices wavering,
humpbacked whales returning,

and Capistrano revealing her
full contralto.
Even the dead Dutch brother gets a petal

on the Asiatic Dayflower. I go
to a day sale
at the dollar store to dull the ecstasy,

but that turns lubricious and joins
in too, you see.
"No hiding place," she says

before devoting herself to oil painting
and Orthodoxy
in the Balkans. Ghosts fall behind

on the court where we play, not in a zone
but one-on-one,
with cross-checking for good measure.

Maestro, my mistress listens
to "Misterioso,"
but Matisse will not be home for dinner.

We cut spring out
without him.
Happy accidents of the swing.

2. ROADS LEADING BEYOND

Jerusalem Everywhere You Go

—from the spine of National Geographic, *August 2003*

To everyone's surprise, the prophecy of Nostradamus is fulfilled by Amazon tribes
who, with the ferocity of clubs and facial tattoos, destroy Paris,
render it as jagged and dry as the Atacama Desert.
These tribes never consider Alaska,
are beaten to the punch by centuries in regard to your average Maya City,
but in not-so-distant Africa, soldiers go on alert along the border of Zimbabwe.

Robert Mugabe, President of Zimbabwe,
will not abide "enemies of our people" or Amazon tribes.
In his office hangs a 3-D five-color plan of a Maya City,
inspiration for the New Harare, which will outshine Paris.
Meanwhile, Stellar sea lions keep barking and mating on Unalaska
Island, the gray fox hunting in the Atacama Desert.

With new soil reports in hand, President Mugabe orders sand from the Atacama Desert.
The agricultural crisis in Zimbabwe
isn't a matter of overzealous land reform but soil drainage, as in Alaska.
He views war room maps on the movements of Amazon tribes,
who are headed straight for the Strait of Gibraltar after decimating Paris,
leaving it looking like Piedras Negras, a ruined Maya City.

Spondylus, a prized, prosciutto-colored sea shell, comprises the mosaic body of a
        ballplayer in that Maya City.
Sand dunes imitate the twisted, bloated bodies of the dead in the Atacama Desert,
and the silent, dry air betrays nothing of moisture or Paris,
still burning as something arcs across Africa like an arrow toward the heart of
        Zimbabwe,
where Mugabe directs the just-delivered sand to be bagged against the coming
        Amazon tribes.
Dilapidated gun mounts, reminders of WW II, remain on Attu Island in Alaska,

but not even these, refurbished and sent to Mugabe from the people of Alaska,
can assure the citizens that their newly won land won't be sacked like a Maya City.
They beat plowshares back into swords and stand ready to face the Amazon tribes,
harsh and deadly as the Atacama Desert.
All eyes are on Zimbabwe
as everyone forgets the fate of Paris.

Near the front line, soldiers drink beer, smoke, and listen to a static-laced broadcast of
    Charlie Parker's "April in Paris"
while Unisea processes its 2.2 million pounds of pollock a day in Alaska.
Then Mugabe breaks in with a speech that rouses even the baobabs to fight for
    Zimbabwe.
Sleeping in pools of sweat to the roar of howler monkeys near a ruined Maya City,
an archaeologist dreams of a great battle, like a sand storm in the Atacama Desert
or the elaborately tattooed and pierced faces of certain Amazon tribes.

But the assault never comes. The Amazon tribes remain as remote as the ruins of Paris
or the sands of the Atacama Desert to the permafrost of Alaska.
They disappear like certain Maya Cities, never to deface the New Jerusalem of
    Zimbabwe.

—for Julie

Nomads with Samsonite

Eels are catadromous, salmon
anadromous. Swallows leave for Capistrano
from the south before the cold constricts
their narrow pink throats,
and dogs, left intact, roam
hundreds of miles
for food, sex, the sheer pleasure of motion.
The earth itself, phenomenologically stable,
hums and bucks with constant movement.
Even the universe opens like a tulip
or closes like a fist, I forget
which. Moreover, the study molders,
the bedroom is a wreck, and the scenery
around here's gone thin.
There's no question we should
light out at first light. And what to take?

Decorum dictates we pack light.
Bernoulli's principle
depends on it. So we'll take
your long hair, like a russet kaffiyeh,
to keep us warm, and my long arms
to serve as sundial, compass,
sign flags to the locals. A bit of rouge,
a sundress, a burnoose, we will go
like this, loose, at day break when
dew sparks on spider's radar.

And we shall take our tongues, all
six tongues—your deep, southern
French one that says, *J'ai besoing du paing*,
and your educated, scientific,
standard American English one.
Who knows when we will need to diagnose
mural folliculitis or order sulfamethoxazole
from the local *farmacia*. And we'll take
my tongues: thimble of Bulgarian, clay cup
of Hindi, water pitcher of Nepalese,
and plate of French, preferably with
my foot in it. Nothing is so necessary

to the alchemy of good travel as
miscommunication or the misreading of maps.

And as for my long, mendacious,
poetic one, let's bury it in the garden
in hopes that it will grow into something
edible while we're gone, or feed it to the dogs
on our way out the gate so they will *bark*
onomatopoeically at neighbors, burglars.
And where to go?

North, south, east, west,
it matters not, just that we move.
Cold is good for health, warm salt water best,
but step by step by step, we're bound to improve.

THE POET AT SEVENTEEN

—after Levis after Rimbaud

His youth echoes with the mechanical whir
of an Italian bicycle in motion over the back roads
he traversed, too disciplined, believing his shaved,
muscled legs starred with ingrown hairs would carry him

like sails. All day outside, the Oklahoma summer
brought out the olive tint in his skin, said to be left
by some Gaul good at building actual bridges
despite leaving only a pier in his father's heart. Leafing

through cycling journals in the dim, artificial cool of his room,
he imagined this absent grandfather architect as hailing
from Normandy, birthplace of Jacques Anquetil, 5-time winner
of *Le Tour*. His father had Anquetil's fine nose

and financed weekends racing in Ft. Worth, Wichita,
Moline. The team met at Love's Country Stores, slept at Motel Six.
Oh, the cultural education, like a trucker's! On Sundays
after races, muscles sore but content unlike his head,

he'd return with a bit of prize money or a new jersey.
Café Columbia: good climbers. *7-11*: American hopefuls.
La Vie Claire: the champions. And he felt safe then, knowing
how to take a corner at speed—the setup, how far to lean,

the exiting arc. He was even happy in his routine, rising
at 6 a.m. to ride a couple hours before school, or during summer,
the lunch shift at a French restaurant in a strip mall,
the only place that would give him long weekends off.

Leaving early, he'd avoid his parents and his neighbors
while the façade of each suburban home sang only to him. Every day
another day to sprint to town limit signs, get caught in rain storms,
and come home drenched and worn, hungry as a beggar.

And on weekends with no races, Jimmy, the team coach,
drove his old yellow Chevy Cavalier at 30 m.p.h. with the hatchback
propped up while he and his teammates motor-paced behind, tucked
into the slipstream. "It's how they get fast on the Continent!"

Jimmy would roar over the classical station blaring on the cheap speakers,
his grease-patinaed hands punctuating the tempo on the dash
as the smell of dope and espresso got churned into the air
rushing by them. Once, he felt too strong for the pace, left

the safety of the draft and raced up alongside the car,
trying to equal its speed on his own. Head tucked low, mouth
gulping air like a dying catfish on some red earth shore,
he couldn't keep up and had to duck back into the slipstream.

At least he had that kind of determination then and welcomed
the physical world while feelings remained orphaned. Girls?
He wore the odd luck of the disinterested and dated
some attractive ones, but his blushing ambivalence

ended most nights early. Their scent on his skin
he'd cover with Lycra the next morning to carry with him
like a mantra for a hundred miles. With the blind faces
of homes behind him and an open, road kill-studded

way before, he felt sure of his ability to escape his beginnings
by sheer muscle power connected to pedals, his weight
suspended over roads leading beyond the borders
of all the earthly and interior maps he knew.

ELABORATE BOARD GAME

A jet moves against the dawn, advances
over the ocean's myriad flora and fauna.
Hydraulics, red and blue wires, and electric
pulses from the green radar screen
that blinks and sweeps like the eye
of a giant abyssal fish
innervate the jet's fuselage.
Inside are organisms who don't
perceive their bodies as moving
525 m.p.h. at 35,000 feet
as long as metal fatigue stays in the future—a detail
in someone else's crash report to distract them
from their quotidian ways
when back home, safely bored over coffee.

Now the dawn advances on the plane, cuts
and peels it off the wall of night
with its ancient accordion music, bellows
smelling of smoke. Slight turbulence shakes
the perfect sleeping hands of passengers
who don't often dream of flying.
They've purchased a reality both more
and less real than their dreams, and dream
of paying in a foreign currency they've practiced
converting. Soon, they'll wake to a morning
seven hours ahead of what they could've had
for free, had they waited.

The taller, cramped, and impatient ones,
unable to sleep, are ready to worship the new light
like a Hindu on the Ganges.
Not because it brings rest or an end to the fatigue
they wear like heavy woolen overcoats,
but because it brings an ability to see,
outside these stuck hours, the waves and clouds
of a planet almost foreign to them now—simple distractions,
like pieces to an elaborate board game,
from the monotony of really flying,
which is not as inspiring as in dreams, weightless,
yet is exactly what they paid for.

RIVER

After a first chai taken from a clay cup
I'd break on the street when done, I'd go to the Ganges,
swim in the warm, silty waters that surrounded my body
like silk, and try not to think about tannery chemicals
from upstream Allahabad or the half-burnt
bodies of the poor who couldn't
afford enough wood to finish the job, even in death.
Amidst midmorning tropical light glinting white
on the monsoon-swollen river's black and tan surface,
children did flips off sandstone columns
near the bathing platform steps, and the last
of late morning worshippers offered
cupped hands of river water to the sun.
We all stayed near the edge lest the current
catch someone and sweep him away to Calcutta.

Often I floated on my back, eyes shut, and imagined
the gently swaying bodies of sadhus, the wandering
holy men of South Asia who, having already died to this world,
don't need to be burnt but are rather tied to rocks
and thrown, whole, into the river. Gently swaying,
like kelp in the ocean, the white Gangetic dolphin
their only witness. And afterwards,
having dried off with a threadbare towel
and the intensifying sun, I'd head back up
the long, ancient steps into the beehive of narrow lanes
filled with rag-tag children, free-roaming, oblivious bovines,
silk shops, hotels, and sweet-meat sellers
to find my favorite samosa stand for breakfast
before another chai in a cup of clay, crushable.

Once, while sitting on a stoop making conversation
in my broken Hindi with the chai wallah, cries
from down the alleyway interrupted and grew
until a dozen women appeared from around the corner
in red, yellow, and green silk saris punctuating their sorrow,
then were gone. Children ran behind delivering the news
in a clipped dialect I had no ear for,
and after they had moved on, the chai wallah
told me one of the women's children had been

swept away while bathing. He said, *Kya Ganga denti hai,*
Ganga lenti, and as I finished my chai, I imagined
being there at that moment, rescuing the child
from a river who takes what she gives. I was that American.

By afternoons in the rundown British Raj-era mansion
in which I'd rented a dark ground-floor room
from a Bengali man named Babu, women
would arrive with newsprint-lined baskets
of fish on their heads and metal balances in their hands.
Babu bought fish for his extended family, but neither I
nor the Australian couple on the top floor cared for flesh.
We'd come to Varanasi, the shining city, to leave
the corporeal world behind. They practiced
Indian classical music on the tablas six hours a day.
I studied Hindi and the poetry of Kabir. We got skinny
while Babu and his family cherished their paunches.

Then I moved from Babu's place to a boatman's three-story
concrete building right on the river. Light flooded my daily existence.
The boatman's family, with its three teen sons, made its living
by muscle, taking tourists in rowboats down the river to the main
bathing and burning ghats, then back. They lived, all seven together,
in a single room downstairs, and rented the others out to tourists
on extended holidays. Above them on the second floor lived
an English couple, both nurses, who'd refashioned their room
like a maharaja's townhouse with embroidered cushions,
hanging silks, and a makeshift bar. There they held elaborate feasts
and consumed only slightly more alcohol than hashish.
Late one night, I heard them fighting at the door over who'd
cheated on whom, and a couple minutes later,
hyenas from across the river answered their cries. Yet many mornings,
they woke long before me to tend to the city's lepers.

I didn't understand that kind of complexity then.
Its beauty was only beginning to dawn on me
like the inflamed, weeping rash given to me by the Ganges
that kept me awake far into the night, or the snippets of racy
dreams about ex-girlfriends despite my nightly meditations on
"compassion for all sentient beings." Sure, I longed for sex
at times but thought it, like socializing, meat, and drugs,
something an aspiring mystic would do best to outgrow.
And so I grew, narrower and narrower like the receding
river in winter, and though my errors shrank, I'd never been
less alive. Anxiety was my ecstasy, dreams my flesh,
longing my bone. *You don't even have any character*
anymore, the monkeys seemed to chide as they stole
my bananas from the windowsill one day.

And then, when Bolinath, my sadhu-like friend, came by
with a knapsack and cried from the shore, "Come with me!
I'm going on a month's pilgrimage," I stood
inert on the balcony though he offered what I'd imagined
my fate to be—something like hydrogen, ethereal and dynamic,
but devoid of the oxygen that makes a live river.

MEDICINE

The doctor wore two days of stubble, an air
of cigarette smoke, and a black Adidas
track suit to dinner, where we drank *rakiya*
out of crystal glasses, each etched with a single
running horse. Enormities lay outside the circle
of kitchen light—wind slamming doors and breaking
glass at night, a young, drunken Bulgarian
who knocked at the wrong apartment and shouted
to let him in, my gut, broken by too many days
in the infectious tropical climate I'd come from,
her dream of me carrying a glowing skull, my need
to escape her, escape me.

The doctor was her friend and sat patiently
while she translated my symptoms.
Who else was there? I can't recall, having
purposefully forgotten so much of our
only winter together in a foreign land.

Somehow, it had all seemed much easier in California
with *temperatures tomorrow again in the 80s*,
cheap Mexican mangos all year round, and our
common tongue. But there, in that intimate land
of saints and demons, broken Romany musicians
playing in the taverns, what looked like a dyslexic
alphabet, and "the blocks"—monoliths of communist
concrete honeycombed with small, indistinct
apartments—we fell sick.

The doctor outlined a plan for me. If I could go
back, that's what I'd ask for—a transplant
of his purpose, the gravity of his dark
features and thick eyebrows, the way he held
a gaze and appeared so relaxed in the relentless cold.
He probably cheated on his wife, but even then,
I could've used the strength of what love
he had for her, even if it was as thin
as the film of brandy left in our glasses after drinking.

Instead, I received a regimen of vitamins, herbal teas,
and dietary restrictions, all of which I ignored.
In place of vitamins, I took indecision and long walks
in the cold. In lieu of herbal teas, alcohol.
And as for diet, the only thing I didn't eat was her,
as I should've, like a bear for warmth during hibernation.

Spring threatened. From our apartment, I witnessed
a black horse gallop down the street pursued by three
men in a car. One leaned out the window
with a rope, but they disappeared around a corner
before he could make the throw.

And when I realized the young, drunk Bulgarian
hadn't had the wrong door, I knew no medicine
would work for us. And when the police came
to ask for my expired passport, it didn't matter
whether we were sick or not—
all the documents agreed I must go.

It was better that way, to go suddenly,
without a big goodbye. Suddenly, like one grows
older and weary of the same fights.
Suddenly, like daylight arrives
after a waning moon's white and gray
arc all night across a bruise-blue sky.

STUDY OF PARIS IN GOOSE LIVER, GLASS, AND RIVER

Not a decision but a millisecond of inattention,
then the *thunk* as the bag hits the street.
His young son parrots his *shit!*, and his wife
scowls, not at his language but at the state of her
foie gras in the now-splintered glass jar, dull yellow fat
seeping into the fissures. Back at their room,
he operates on the delicacy with tweezers
and declares it fit to eat, but her pleasure
is ruined when she cuts her tongue,
the wound like the bite of a hummingbird.

The Jewish children in a playground near the Seine
have forgotten the lugubrious mouth of March's earth
that swallowed so many, unanswered. Two men
on the side speak of language, god, the manners
of French women in bed. The children
play tag and, unlike the men, haven't
forgotten their bodies, don't need a woman to find them again.
J'arrive! they shout, and the words replay
from the mouth of one man to the other about
his lover who narrows her eyes, tenses, and says the same
when she arrives, comes, is there, brilliant
and sweaty like the children on the walk home
down la Rue de Fourcy without the prick
of thorns or barbed wire or sex.

At his lover's apartment (she makes the money),
they drink red wine, smoke hash, and listen
to his electronic music experiments. The visitor
envies his expatriate friend this city of light
as an abode, and this dark woman,
half French, half Serb, flirtatious, generous,
unfaithful, and elegant. Like the city.
Tu es très expérimentée.
He speaks French like his tongue is scarred,
but she likes his literary vocabulary.

Later, man and wife make love against the cold glass
of their hotel room's balcony window.
He envisions them on the surface of the Seine. She
imagines a crane, its white feathers bowing on her skin.

One good day of sun. Many days of rain
as milky gray sky and limestone blend,
and then, a black cloud bringing hail.

The coffee clouded with milk
wakes him from himself. The river laden with silt
drowns him from himself. Her body white as milk
obscures him from himself. The food sautéed in butter
hides him from his ribs who know. The pigeons' coos
break him from terrible silence. His friend's *I saw God*
after passing out and smashing his lover's
glass flower vase as he hit the floor
hides him from his self-abuse.

On the merry-go-round
near the Hôtel de Ville, mirrors
reflect him, his wife, his son,
together and separate, together
and separate again.

The Seine is high this spring,
so they cannot take a boat.
They can walk along the river and speak
of its floods, its liver-gray color,
and its suicides, the splinters
of light in the water reaching
out to them like the arms of a god
to cut their tongues out
and take them for his own.

SPLASH ZONE

We walk onto that godly terrain,
      space of infinite
complexity no map could portray,
      wrought by ocean.
Here a pool of about 2 by 3 feet
      where rock lost
to water. And its denizens:
      156 sea snails,
49 green anemones, 24 rock
      crabs, 17
mussels. (Census figures
      good only
for this one of two daily low tides.)
      Multiply by
thousands but factor in variables (x, y, z)
      for each pool—
nudibranchs, bat stars, abalones, clams,
      surf grass, limpets, spider crabs, isopods,
barnacles, chitons, sea urchins—see, over there, a seal
      sleeping next to
another tide pool while the Pacific grinds
      her tremendous
girdle of water into the outer edges of rock
      around us. Another
seal, "daughter of Lir," peeks from—none
      says it better,
damn his fascism—"glare azure of water"
      at us, really looks!
Sociologically, what is a moment of recognition
      with a seal? I
try not to leer, try to be as coy as the dog
      who rides white
wave wash that would both frost and crush me
      quickly. Tamara
holds a plastic shopping bag open for
      our sons,

who pluck mussels off the rocks
          while two locals
fish for monkey-faced eels and sculpin
          with their long
cane rods and short lines. The Buddhist
          in me hovers
over the bag and picks out the slender black
          talismans of food
that are too rich with other lives
          —tiny anemones,
healthy looking barnacles—to take, but later,
          I purposefully
wade into a deep pool near the edge,
          where sea urchins
have made their beds, find one
          whose bed is not
so deep, and pick it from its spot.
          The spines
brown to gentian violet and not
          so sharp. I
bend them aside and crack
          the test
with a rock to reach the delicate
          orange flesh
tinged with fish and ocean.
          Omnivorous,
but seldom do I kill
          the animals
I eat, and never before have I killed
          such a beautiful
one. *This is life*, I think as I taste
          and see
the water rising at the edge of this
          complexity
we will abandon for terrain
          above the splash zone
before high tide and darkness
          arrive to efface
all trace of us.

SHOWDOWN

—after Loren Goodman

1. Quarterfinals

Wallace Stevens vs. King Kong:
reptile mind defeats
large primate
every time.
Stevens advances.

Virgil vs. Dante:
after some rabbit punches
and table sandwiches, Dante
recovers to beat Virgil with woods,
win in extra rounds.
Virgil to Eighth Circle. Dante advances.

Emily Dickinson vs. a fly:
no contest.
Fly dies.
Emily advances.

The Italian Peninsula vs. the Indian Subcontinent:
boot kicks a bag of one billion—
half a billion jump out of the bag
onto the boot. Boot sinks as UN
heli-lifts the Uffizi to Tirana.
India advances.

2. Semifinals

Dante vs. Stevens:
Stevens puts on the mind of a snowman,
but Dante uses rain of fire.
Stevens throws garbage, like *the* and *and,*
from the dump at him. Dante
weaves them into terza rima.
Stevens uses volcano.
Dante counters with beatific vision.
Dante wins. Stevens agrees to go to church
next Sunday morning.

Emily Dickinson vs. Indian Subcontinent (with half
its population): Emily tries insanity. India eats
her derangement, shits marigolds. Emily becomes reclusive.
India shows up in her shower. Emily
tries silence. One *mauni* outsilences her.
Emily leaves Amherst for Mumbai and opens
an arranged marriage service.
India advances.

3. Finals

India vs. Dante:
India posts up and blocks the lane.
Dante clears the puck. India lands
a left jab via the Punjab. Dante
evokes Beatrice. India evokes Valmiki
and Kalidasa. Dante resorts to Satan.
India makes Satan another deity.
Dante prays.
India has tea.
After a short scrum,
Dante succumbs
to amoebic dysentery.
India wins and makes him
pedal rickshaws in New Delhi.

Dante bilks the tourists every day.

BARABAIG, LOSING LAND IN NATIVE TANZANIA, CONSIDER WASHINGTON STATE

—from the spine of National Geographic, *July 2004*

The sun
needs no cocaine
to run its brain as it hides from Olympic Park.
The elephant-hunting Barabaig
of Tanzania and wind scorpions
sacrifice more to it than a Moche priest in a Peru Temple,
or the retirees in Nalcrest, FL.

No dogs wake in Nalcrest, FL,
to the sun.
They're forbidden, along with Peru Temple-
style sacrifices of softball game losers, and cocaine.
Wind scorpions,
while not forbidden, are as rare there as Olympic Park
rain and redwoods. Tuesdays are Barabaig

Bingo, Thursdays Coral Society, Fridays Barabaig
Bar-B-Que Night. Mmmmm, Nalcrest, FL,
redolent with roasting elephant again. Olympic Park's
horsetail, hedge nettle, and salmonberry smell similar when the sun
warms them, which it seldom does. Wind scorpion?
Tastes like chicken, not elephant. But the aftertaste is like Peru Temple
prisoner pre-sacrifice cottonmouth. Not as pleasant as cocaine.

A Moche priest adorned in gold silt and glimmering like cocaine
on a mirror in July's meager shade slit throats like the Barabaig
dismember the gray elephant after a hunt. Peru Temple
sites such as Huaca Cao Viejo harbor the victims' bones while Nalcrest, FL,
hosts the "old bones" that remain alive, some as brittle as a dead wind scorpion's
exoskeleton, some still as pliable as an Olympic Park
vine maple and staying that way with the sun's

vitamin D-eliciting kiss, like the sun
is out on cocaine
or something. Why're ya back near Olympic Park
already, ya jerk sun? We're done with you like the Barabaig
have no use for elephant guns—spears, baby, spears. Wind scorpions
don't hear, exactly, but feel, as you feel with the Peru Temple
of your ear. Retired ears in Nalcrest, FL,

have nothing to fear save the deafening bite of alligators in Nalcrest, FL.
Astronomers, seeking a different perspective, walk on the sun
after sacrificing themselves inside Peru Temples.
Their astral bodies the color of cocaine,
they move through space like wind scorpions
and possess the fecundity of all the flora in Olympic Park,
the bravery of the Barabaig.

The sun is the giant yellow elephant they hunt like the Barabaig,
on foot, for days, no food or water, only spears. Nalcrest, FL,
is close to Kennedy, where they monitor such astronomers and Olympic Park
marijuana fields, hidden under mist from normal surveillance and the sun
that dawns, golden as a wind scorpion,
and feeds the bloodless friezes on the sides of Peru Temples
their actual daily dose of astral cocaine.

In truth, the sun, source of all energy on earth, needs cocaine
occasionally, like Olympic Park needs occasional sun, Barabaig
spear-throwing contests, wind scorpions, and Peru Temple
replicas to inspire some to retire there, not in flat, sunny Nalcrest, FL.

3. Elsinore

THE INEBRIATE AIRPLANE

Humanity was putting shoes on the huge child Progress.
—Louis-Xavier De Ricard (A. Rimbaud)

As I flew through disenfranchised, friendly skies,
I felt the plane out of the control
of redneck pilots who'd surmised
the hijacker with ice picks—one for each eye—a fool.

Oxygen masks dropped and flight attendants distributed the balm
of peanuts and small vodkas as we, released from Bernoulli's principle,
plummeted. Vomit filled the space between the Twenty-third Psalm
and breathing as heavy as a rutting couple's. I—the only disciple

who'd singularly spotted the sun's moldy eye
through the cabin windows and aligned the wave
of our fall with the approaching storm—dodged the artificial dye
of bleeding seat backs that gave

commercial airline colors to the faces of passengers
as they sank from my vision, the bodies of drowned sailors
who believed too much in the fall. Was I a cur
to believe the craft's rise into the torpor

of a nuclear Asiatic sky, its belly the color
of Buddha? And why did I miss nothing
of those terrible dinners with impossibly cold spoons to stir
the mousseline of cooks' bloods or the jabbering

mouths of children standing in their seats? The terminal
hung so far below like an old dryer at a dump
and would never again be a place to muddle
about while eyeing fashion porn's rump

and décolletage on glossy covers. The cabin
witnessed my terror of freedom and offered to strip
its metal skin like a serpent or dancer in
a nightclub of clouds. Exposed to the rip

of the wind, my eyeballs froze with vision. Strangely,
the landing gear stayed in three sets of four
beneath the airplane floor's transparency
while squealing their cries of clemency for

my life. Never trust landing gear. The engines
no longer hummed or whined, but their lift
remained like the sensation in the groin of indigenous
children swinging by a river. The immediate rift

between all flight patterns and this pure sailing
that approached the speed of C. I'd escaped gravity
and could only cry ice for the thud of falling
bodies at the nadir. Space's space made levity

in place of my disintegrating body—the weakness
of the arms, nausea, radiation poison of violet
pulsation. Someone new grew inside made not of flesh
but airy desire and expression, the end of violent

fear. This open vessel made of metal and I
had nothing to do with stars but occupied the subliminal
bruise-blue space between the Devouring Eye
and thighs splashed red by birth. Under the lintel

of a million deities, I saw sin as the tree
that it was, rootless, and felt my desire for everything.
The pure sensation of interment and sodomy
filled my nerve set like the invasive whining

of swine. Like a demon, I was cast out in replication
and thereby cast out my swine while the apex of nowhere
arrived quickly from its previous location
of one second before to hit me square

in the chest with phantasms of orange and purple
that ran through hotter than Master Gerveys's colter.
Inexorably, the gaseous vista opened from its furl
and snapped in my face. Not all the fervor

of Chenrezig's eyes could've absorbed such light,
and my sight went as dark as the hair of that woman
from Abyssinia with a dulcimer. I became a slight
embryo or infant suckling. From that moment, like a stamen,

I gather memory's pollen as it spirals through
in whorls like the hair on an infant's crowning head.
Agony was absolutely absent and Einstein's equation grew
into my own extralucidity. The universe hummed a bed

of torch in my spine like a laboring engine on fire.
The earthly spectrum was eaten like so many peanuts,
and a black and white rainbow revealed the spire-
like height of my insouciance, like an earthworm's

dream of wine. Nothing could humble the opalescent,
ethereal flies of my organs as they landed smack
on God's eyes, which had never had the scent
of an atheist so close. The seasons' back-

ward progression to a pure summer there in the midst
of what can be so cold told me nothing of the Old Life
or the New World but rather of Life itself, kissed
by materiality with no strife,

a conjunction. If I missed anything of the New World
from where this flight had left, it was the space
between riffs in "Crazeology" as it whirred
over the endless hangover caused by the pace

of such a desperate state, and when I returned
to the terminal like a pigeon from ash, the hollow eyes
there made me resolve not to be churned
back in, nor to buy our winging lies.

HAMLET'S MEDITATION

It makes nothing, this world, just empty return
upon itself like snow that snows and blots
out the surface roots of a tree. Windburn

dogs a woman out for a jog who knots
her eyes looking for the cross light. She sees
and goes. The slush will slick the road tonight

for a wreck, but now in the gutter a dull sluice seizes
the day. Hurray. How our lives go, even
in lightest Italy, where marble friezes

pit from pollution and fathers caress forgiven
parish members too closely. *When in Rome . . .*
Erasure. The Bosnian street boy, driven

to thieving, when caught near the Hippodrome
has the presence to say, *Non faccio niente!*
And later, when snow falls on the Pantheon's dome,

he goes for shelter in that grand space of nothing.

OPHELIA'S DREAM

Late at night, our feet rhyme
like buttons on a shirt.
First, the tops of mine
cupped in your arches, supine.
Then, your arches, prostrate,
over the tops of mine. Points
of contact change with position,
rhythm, but always the firm
metatarsi, the warm, taut
skin over the flex of the tendons,
and the delicate hairs on the toes,
brushed and brushing.

HAMLET'S LETTER FROM EXILE

Dear Ophelia, I miss your ways with scrimshaw,
the delicate play of wrist over dull walrus
tusk for months till gleaming white fetishes
fell into our bed like solder from acetylene.
First, a school of Ozark Mountain fish to recall
your home: O Minnow, O Emerald Shiner, O
Missouri Saddle Darter, O Common Shiner,
O Hornyhead Chub. Then, the effigy of me. Finally,
a dinghy in miniature, an ivory-clothed ivory man
reared back with his impossibly thin spear
aimed at the heart of a whale. We were a circle of three
in the gloam of the oil lamp there by the looted
sea—you, me, our sculpted life in ivory.

OPHELIA IN *THE ABYSS*

It's not the drink that knocks me out,
it's the swallow, the anesthetizing gulps
of wave after wave of this vaguely salty
neon orange fluid, like something
out of a dentist's office.
Usually, only the dead know
how many swallows it takes
to get to the center, fill the lungs,
drown, ah, not sleep but a flailing
before the body convulses upon itself
like a sea worm on a dock in July.
But I know now too and I can tell you—no,
no more "seems"—put your hand to my throat
and count the rhythmic rise and fall of those
delicate rings: one, two, three, four—
you count, I've done this before, this reverse
of birthing, this ingestion so one can live
at great depths, not give at every step.

> *FBS, or Fluid Breathing System, was developed by the US Navy in an attempt
> to put live divers at unprecedented depths. An oxygenated fluorocarbon
> emulsion that can be "breathed," it not only serves as a substitute for traditional
> SCUBA equipment but also puts internal pressure on the lungs, which keeps
> them from collapsing.*

See, Hamlet and I had many babies and hid them
in the castle. When the king's men went to retrieve
my father's body, one even crawled out from beneath the stairwell.
He'd been suckling at the wound—attention to feedings
was never my strength—and scrambled over to the curtains
to wipe his mouth, then disappeared.
Their names? Why, Rosemary, Pansy, Fennel, and Columbine,
Rue, Daisy, Flopsy, Mopsy, and Indigo. Equally boys'
and girls' names all. But once Hamlet became more bent
on revenge than bottle feeding or nappy changing, I too
gave them up to run wild in the castle, surviving
on the odd dropped tart or drumstick and cute begging tricks,
or lichen when desperate. Most will make it given my sturdy
servant-to-the-king stock and their father's wits. And I,
rejected and rejecting, must go to the abyss

and defuse the nuclear warheads sent to destroy
peaceful, amorphous aliens.

> *Yesterday, unnamed sources leaked that a US Navy nuclear submarine had
> sunk into the Challenger Deep of the Marianas Trench, where sights of
> luminous bodies were being investigated as a possible alien conspiracy to steal
> our technology. The Navy is denying the report and related rumors that they
> would solve the issue with a tactical nuclear strike, which some fear might set
> off earthquakes and tsunamis.*

You thought I'd really drown? With a dress like that,
I could've hidden enough oxygen to swim
underwater to the Baltic Sea, but all I had to make
was the Zodiac around the bend, where Navy SEALs,
strong, decisive men, waited with towels, hot coffee,
and a Life Suit, orange unfortunately not my best color.
And damn if they didn't turn away when I changed,
but no one stared or blushed either. A strange new
space, this liminal not object but not quite subject.
They whisked me to a helicopter, which flew me here,
and now, high-tech helmet on and salty,
oxygenated drink swallowed, I'm the center
of attention, an unknown agent going to the abyss,
secret mission to myself.

> *The frequency and use of X, or unknown, agents is difficult to discuss by its
> very design, but historically known examples that involved such operatives
> include the invasions of North Africa and Normandy in WW II and the
> overthrow of numerous communist regimes in Central and South America in
> more recent times, showing their vast historical and political puissance.*

My dive suit is filled with heated water like the tropics
in a castle. My helmet is screwed on tight, my lungs full
of elixir, and I step into the lighted circle of water
inside the Navy submersible on the edge of the trench
and sink, more weighted than buoyant, more
toothed whale than woman, the hair above my sex becoming
seaweed as I descend. There is the sensation
of falling, yes, and the pressure does increase—my temples
ache, my arms and legs feel as if a million rasping hagfish
feed there. I pass out at one point and wake to the perpetual
slow-motion fall. *H, I never loved you either* is the bell
that rings in my head, answered by the antiphony, *Father,
go suck the king's cock.* Suddenly, I'm more me than ever
and never more alone or distant from the light. I'm
mollusk, and cradled on my body, the pearl for which
I've traded the world.

Still denying rumors of a nuclear submarine's encounter with aliens in the Pacific, the Navy maintained that its invasion of the Volcano Islands was protective in nature and designed to strengthen, not undermine, US-Japan relations.

Sure, I defused the warheads (save the one
I put in my pack), greeted the aliens (not nearly
as interesting as me, who seems solid but is amorphous
in reality as opposed to their on-the-sleeve fluidity),
and pulled the cord to inflate the BC vest
that hugged my chest and brought me back.
I even held onto a buff sailor as I coughed the fluid
out of my bruised lungs and shuddered through
to the respiration of air. Then I noticed the sailor
had breasts and commanded a nearby man
to fetch me a blanket, and I thought the descent
had changed something. But there were queens
in my time, and women who held enormous influence
on the court. Here power was the ability
to command a man who would later scan
the artificial breasts and shaved pubes of glossy
female forms while in the head? Ah, to Elsinore,
I'm as good as dead, and the confines
of this fucking sub hurt my head.

I, Ophelia of the Abyss, pearl of wisdom
in my mouth and nuclear warhead in my pack,
will ditch this vessel at first port, commandeer
a low-drawing sloop and be three times the pirate
Blackbeard or John Avry ever was. My flag?
On a field of black, Jolly Roger
with red *yantra* of Kali underneath.
If you see it, tremble—I'm strong, fashionable,
and mean, and know mercy is best extended
to oneself. If not, one is as good as dead.
Once I have a sizeable crew, I'll return to Elsinore,
call my children to my ship, raze the cold castle,
then sail to Fiji.

And when I lay my children down
to sleep, I'll tell them my story.

The pearl and warhead will illuminate their dreams.

4. THE COMEDY OF LIGHT

Arboreal

The trees planted in
the median
follow me. They

could be a kind of peppertree
given the narrow,
delicate leaves, like

children's fingers, the milky-white
sap, and berries
with a spicy resinous smell.

I try not to look at them,
but there they are,
flaming red and asking

for my attention. The mind's
luminosity
adheres to such things

and makes the world leap
into being.
Without the world, consciousness

shines in the dark cave of
your skull
and can implode or enlighten

depending upon your ease
with such light.
But the alternative—perception,

parsing things up, then labels,
and finally,
the schematic diagrams of the brain—

so often seems an ego trick
to make the little
you feel essential, or in need of

a new car. Or an education.
A friend
is reading Ricoeur in translation.

(Ricoeur's words denser than daylight
is long, so he could
still be reading, though I suspect

you understand "is reading"
as "read."
Don't you know we grow old

through such interpretations?
Couldn't it all be
present progressive?)

I'm dubious about anything
in translation,
especially French

literary theory, and wonder
about the hours
he spends grinding his mind,

delicate blossom, through such
machinations.
Such precious time could be

better spent in the parking lot
contemplating
the essential red

of the trees, manifested
seemingly
without translation.

TRIWEEKLY CIMARRON RIVER REPORT, MAY 17TH TO AUGUST 28TH

High and tumultuous, medium and running, *dulce et decorum
nella sulla bankula*, ethereal and brown, murky but clearer
than the Arkansas, Cimarron red, frothy and shimmering,
vaguely blue, silvery and verdant, pensively dark green, aquasienna,
milk teeth blue, frothy and stringy red, khaki, pimento
and bass, greyhound green, crimson but given to viridescence,
lapis lazuli, steel brown, interstate blue, shimmering taupe,
recycled white glass, slate, macadam, invisible, tree bark, shivering
liver, café au lait, minnow, chiffon, raspberry margarita,
month-old caramel apple, lady of the lake green and silver,
manure, milky vermeil, catfish belly and roiling, invisible,
brick house, Serengeti red, gravy spleen, cattle, basalt.

SCOPE

The round eye of the classroom building,
crosshatched with muntins
and set in a red brick gable
wet with sunlight under an ocean
of October atmosphere,
mimics a periscope. The pressure
of engines starting, students, wide-eyed
with love or heartbroken, and a confrontation
over illegal parking will not
break the hull of the building as it glides
through exhalations,
inhalations of warm and
cold fronts. The climate of depth,
the brain and what
it won't say, bricks,
vents, and windows.
We enter the submarine
for classes of a set duration.
Then, release.

*

A young woman in tight slacks
with a faux snakeskin print cuts
down the library steps
toward the union. A young man
watches her cross the space
between buildings
in the late afternoon light.
He thinks of an orange, Picasso's
blue period, how they could
never get along as long as he's allergic
to nail polish, fearful of snakes and polyester.
Still, he wonders whom she loves.

*

A flock of heron-like birds
heads south. The ones in back
rotate to the front of the loose arrow,

silently sharing the work as they go.
Another man stops and looks up too.
"Too bad I don't have my gun," he says.
The bells
ringing in the tower
are prerecorded.

*

We could leave the paper blank
and call it *#37 in Light Gouache*,
but the retina would continue to register
subtle shifts of light, shadow,
and last night's dream
of an overdue library book
found in the aquarium. "There is
no there there," but there is,
always, something to be seen. Trees
are good for wonderment over
intricacy—each leaf
with a stem, each stem attached
to a branch, every branch flowing
back to the trunk, and finally,
down into the soil, a source
of dignity.

EL HOMBRE MUERTO

Bicycle ride to the east,
back country tarmac.
A turkey vulture rises off
something dead, a raccoon on its side,
fur peeled back, vibraphone
of ribs in the stark sun, archipelago
of gore born from its interior
onto the hot black sea.

Raccoon, dead on the road, strange
omen you are, masked and split
open. Hit in the dark no doubt.

Five miles on, my head still has him,
an Athena in Zeus's aching temple.
I enter. He's there, body still splayed apart
but animated. He ambles up
and opens his mouth, a beautiful
red velvet purse from which I pluck
two perfect gold coins, one
for each eye.

SHACKLETON'S CREW MEMBER WRITES FROM GRAD SCHOOL

We survive by the tail of the dog.
I won't mention the flanks or testes
because the nights we eat those
are not survival—we're alive then.
Stuck on this ice floe, where the energy is
frozen. And all together, like a pack of penguins
or scholars. We being the latter.

The headaches from the glare are the worst.
One member thinks of cranial trepanation. Others
focus on licking ice off Shackleton's black boots
while the eyelets of his boots watch them as they lick
all together, like a choir, except
no one can sing. The wind's one long voice last winter
sounded nothing like song. But we survive
our pessimism, even make our own vellum to record
insights about headaches and ice.

There are soccer matches and departmental parties, too.
More to be looked forward to than another toe falling off
or another lecture by Shackleton and the faculty he's become
on endurance and enthusiasm for the life of a penguin.
Even so, all the members practice, at night in secret,
their waddles, and when they get good, they practice
in groups. The few dogs we haven't eaten
howl at the dark shapes coming closer,
then going away, then coming closer again.

Go off and be a dog by yourself, fuck
this penguin business, I thought one day.
The snow burned my hands and knees
as I crawled toward the south. Hypothermia
and delirium overtook me, and I became a podium,
then a dog, then a woman
who offered my former form's muzzle
all the parts of her body rhyming with bliss.
So as not to get my fur sticky, I ate each piece
carefully, but when I came to, dressed as a man,
the blood from my frostbitten hands

had stiffened the fur on my parka. At least the mates
who found me didn't eat me.

It's dark now. I write by keys: the wind's
one long drone, the whine of two dogs,
the squeak of boots on snow, the skin of something
being made into vellum, and someone thinking,
low and pregnant, like an orange. I will seal this
in a bottle with wax from my last candle
and cast it toward the moon that glows like my
numb body but wanes much colder.
A sign. The comedy of light is never lost on us,
who live in a circle of ice and frigid
sea water, dogs' blood and ideas
that roll around like oranges, like the sun.

HAGIOGRAPHY AND HANGING

My friend regards himself in a crescent
of broken mirror before class
when he wants to look his best berating our

"inescapable Puritan heritage." I don't know
who broke the mirror, and I believe in
no destiny. If you study hagiography, you'll see

miracles trump work. St. Anselm spoke with the birds.
St. Jerome juggled flaming roses, no ash.
St. Theresa made it with G., bathed

in ecstasy. Of course, whole towns sometimes converted
to sainthood through ergot on the wheat.
Entire villages shared brain's fire and shutter.

So what's up with Salem? A tear in the sackcloth
of too much sense to let some dark light in—?
and then, nothing, just sales. "Today, the city's products

include cables, flashbulbs, games, lamps, plastics,
radio tubes, tannery and leather products, and valves."
Note: We didn't burn them, we hanged them.

Nineteen people to be exact. Somehow it seems
easier on my mind with fire, knife of flame
on their shins, bellies, breasts. The body devoured,

the myth of the phoenix. "You know what Cocteau says?"
my friend asks. "Don't look in a mirror
to see yourself, look at your life." Or our lies, I think.

Like *I* is not another, is different than *we.* Or belief
in some sanctity of fire over a cold gray rope, tight
on a woman's throat, choking out herbal

folk remedies, unpatentable shadow language
grounded in the absolute symbolism of flowers
and roots, bowing to no god. Better we regarded

our images in fragments instead of silvering
new mirrors. Better we understood our logic
of rope, our fantasies of fire.

Central Hockey League Night

Before the contest, the arena's halls
and maculate concrete floors
echo the roiling, unintelligible polyphony

of a crowd excited. Between periods,
or during, children, released
from the adult spectacle, return with miniature

plastic hockey sticks for pickup games.
Their intricate scrum near concessions recalls
a drawing of an eighteenth-century

Iroquois lacrosse match. Deeper inside the arena,
the crowd surrounds the ice with a studied
intensity, like medical students at an anatomy lesson,

and the light is sterile white tinged with blue,
the color of mother's milk. The crowd
is of one, maybe two, minds. It stands

for the allegiance and an early fight
in which the visiting team's player gets it
right on the chin, goes down hard.

Many rise for refreshments and return
to masticate peanuts, nachos, and pizza
from thick, delicate, hairy, manicured, slight,

and greedy hands while beer sloshes
down gullets, down stairs. On the ice,
players give as much as young men

with a limited future in a sport can. They earn
30K a season, which isn't bad unless you consider
the likelihood of taking a puck in the teeth

or drawing a bigger, more embittered
opponent in a fight. Or ash-tree stick
across the back of the neck, 10-hour stinking

bus ride for a 5-game series on the road,
homeless. The lucky ones end up coaches
or managers by 35, but tonight the crowd

gets them all confused with luck
when the home team goes up by 3
in the 3rd period of play, and the youngest

children's faces wear the anonymity of sleep
like a classic goalie's mask. The red
and blue lines, immobile in the rink's ice,

cannot be erased but will
melt after the game to reveal
the poker-faced concrete beneath.

LOTTO

One's lot in life
determines a lot.

A shitty lot in life?
Overlooking the freeway,
or on a toxic Superfund site,
or just too ghetto.

A friend wants to buy
a better lot in life—
a plot of land in the mountains
of Bulgaria.

We have a nice lot
despite the lack
of mountains.

Fall in a parking lot
because the legs
you find yourself with
fail you, are run through
with the spider veins of age.

A lot of things can save you: someone
to pick you up and drive you around,
a TV of infinite distraction, pharmaceuticals,
and cash, lots of it.

Don't count on Lot's wife.
Her salty kiss only brings
copious tears. Lots.

I'd like to live near alotawater,
like the Pacific or the Atlantic
or the Adriatic. Dead Sea
dead last on the list, which
has lots of other options, so.

Don't piss on your lot
if you live in the city. Okay

in the country. The same goes for
parking on your lot.

War is not a lot of fun.
Neither is torture.
A bad lot of them took him
into the building,
and when he came out,
he was alive but no longer
cared much to live.

Your lot fits into a puzzle
of millions of lots, and bumps
and grinds up against them
like a pebble on an ocean
shore, and affects them
deeply, like love and hate
and lots of other subtle
variations on those emotions.

Watch your lot. Tend it.
Don't curse it unless you must.

The lot of many equals a lot
of great loss with briars
and rules binding their
greatest desires—to see
the city's destruction
and live, to kiss the wrong
rightly, to bring down
the lot of greed that makes
ruins of so many good plots.

SURVIVAL

Conscription for all bears,
polar bears in particular.
> —Mark Parsons, "Leave"

Conscription, eh? What about invasion
of the grizzly bear's land by humans
and an occasional escaped polar bear?
Despite being able to, professional wrestling style,
body slam a cow carcass to the ground
just to break its bones and get to the marrow,
everyone knows *Ursus arctos horribilis*
is never a match for *Ursus maritimus.*
Something about the isolation
frames the polar bear
harder. Still, there's the issue of survival,
not just defeating somebody
but adapting the palate and range
to what's there, thereby growing large.
Not just in body. "When I put on the mask,
I become the bear," says George Taylor
of the Le-La-La Dancers as his wife
sits next to him looking
apprehensive. A grizzly must eat
enough calories to live on stored fat
for half-a-year, and the diet includes
cattle, salmon, army cutworm moths,
trash from dumpsters, and the faces
of errant humans. *Just a tiny piece,*
chewing on it slowly. Consider it
an honor to be disfigured and left alive,
touched by such an adaptable species,
as if the four-inch claws were
sacred ivory combs. Survival
is not horrible to the one surviving.
Consider that some grizzlies
interact in complex ways with their captors
instead of merely biting off heads
and tossing uniformed bodies around
on a concrete slab painted white
to simulate the floes of the Arctic.
Two colors—white and red.
Grizzlies work a palate of earth shades.

"Where their claws contour the ground,
they plant seeds and release scarce nitrogen
from lower soil levels." Their feces,
rich with digested grubs and fish,
and the carcasses of their kills,
become earth. They're "heavyweight gardeners,"
"ecosystem accelerators." By comparison, what
do vast expanses of ice and ocean need
save a witness of equally incomprehensible
being. Colorless, quill-like hair.
They are not of this world.
While grizzlies are about dialogue,
even if that means they eat your face,
subtly, without you noticing they've been
sleeping next to you at night, going
to your classes, your bars, your zoos,
demeaning themselves into trained actors,
or permitting the cameras of over 200 visitors a day
to click and whir while they eat, thank you.
Of course, it would be easier to just
have a system of conscription
and know you don't belong.
No take over from the inside, no
confusion about roles, who's on top,
keystone species. But that's not
the kind of survival I'm talking about here.
I'm talking about being alive.

Your life is in your own hide.

5. ALL OTHER UNITIES

PAST LIFE DRIFT

Their meeting? The sound
of a drawer of cutlery drawn open
quickly, jangled. The nerve
set infinite, fresh cut fig on a
holographic plate. East Jerusalem,
1967, he knew they'd met before,
but it was queer this
realignment of eyes when not disguised
by gun scopes.
The sight of her bare breasts.
Blam, blam.
The Red Sea taste
on his skin. And holy was the rifle,
the matzo, and the sin.

IN PROGRESS

Your immanence, like a rusted hound,
St. Bernard Mastiff shrunk in rain
to Poodle Pekingese. The road was long. And winding.
Windy too. And your knees knocked
on the tarmac as you fell from da feet
to da chest and da hands. "Kiss my black
gravel barrel, suck tarry wind," it sang.
You really should run more often, you
thought in anagram. "You" disguised
as me, which means *oui*.

Dear Anselm, let's call my daily life
Vermeer, my other life Goya. One
bathed with quiet light as a figure toils
making *crêpes dentelles*, the other
the impact of being shot in a gauzy white shirt
while the mouth of night gnaws
on my head. Furthermore, dawn and dusk
have been as subtle as buzz saws lately,
motoring across the sky of a consciousness
etched clean of words.

Summer always finds us—I, you, him, her,
the Proteus lie of pronouns. The protons
clear valance sounds like a recorded,
scratchy bell. My head's not right, right?
Ring on the third stop, exit
the diesel beast and climb the splintered,
garrulous steps to the top. Stop. Ring again.
The thing that opens is a door.
The thing that opens what opens
is me. No verse, straight on.

GENEALOGY

Difficult to figure, like a town named Moore
with a yellow happy face painted on its gunmetal-gray
water tower and just slightly fewer pregnant high schoolers
than Trans Ams and Camaros. That was their hometown.
And on a street like the edge of a postage stamp
lost behind the coffee pot for months, torn and ticked
with food particles, they lived.

Once, I dreamt I was there with my roly-poly
disco queen aunt, who taught me how to read
when not washing her own children's
"foul mouths" out with the pink foaming action
of Mr. Bubble. It was always *Saturday Night Fever*
on Queensbury Street, and The Bee-Gees sang
with a penetrating whine while my aunt and I tried
desperately to catch a wasp in an old mason jar.
It never landed on the record player's dust-covered
dust cover, and when it stung her, I knew she would die.

I can't remember whether I dreamt this
before or after she actually died. Definitely after
I learned the meaning of *orgasm* and *fellatio*
from her nurse's encyclopedia and fancied myself,
through that moment of study, older and wiser
even though I was really as confused as if I'd read
the ritual for becoming a 33rd Degree Mason
or the recipe for *tiramisù*. But knowledge
is power, even when it arrives too soon
or too late. Like my aunt, a nurse, learned
the prescription drugs she abused
had hardened her lungs to the consistency
of water-logged bracket fungus on a tree.

Of course, no one knew then that her husband,
like Hephaestus with his polio limp and affections
of wrought iron, would die watching ESPN while inhaling
the last bits of life from oxygen tubes in his nose
and cigarettes from a green and blue package
suggesting the sea. I'll never forget
how well dressed his undertakers were as they

straightened the stiffening body to the gurney's
horizontal cut, the man in a charcoal suit
and dress shirt with cufflinks, the woman in a sheer
white blouse that seemed luminescent and left her
cleavage tastefully visible. And then their eldest son,
my cousin, dreamt inside the same clapboard house
of becoming lupine while the hungry mouth of a tumor
devoured his insides. And now their youngest son
holds down the same house's front porch
with sacks of empty aluminum beer cans. I'd prefer
to pronounce the above as "aluminium,"
just for the sake of distance.

We are maternal blood relatives, and try as I might
to uncover my special, royal, paternal dispensation
from addiction, suicide, arson, and that simple
daftness of the jaywalking kind,
I cannot. And lately, after certain
trying hours with myself or my sons,
I've been thinking of washing my own
mouth out with soap, abusing my wife's
prescription veterinary products,
or sucking on straw, gravel, or my lip until some gist
of what seems like life comes out. Then I take
a long walk around our property with its edges
frayed like those of an old postcard from a distant country
showing pigs prized for their ability to sniff out
truffles from the earth, and I say *merde!* three times
aloud, and it is done. I belong to no one.

CRÊPES DENTELLES

In fourth grade, I played a Civil War martyr
whose closing epistolary monologue
effaced all others. My mother sewed for weeks
to make the navy felt fit handsomely,
and Directors A. Lincoln and J. Racine
lauded me publicly. This was before mother
assassinated father, and the doughy
belly of love, with its thick,
yeasty smell, filled the kitchen.
Pancakes instead of crêpes.

The half fridge with its stainless steel door,
like an appliance in the galley of an aircraft,
hid the body through the trial
until it was jailed for rot.
"Habeas corpus," said the pontiff.
"Ooooooh!" came the collective surprise
from the rows of parishioners who swooned
like iron stamens beneath the feet
of magnetic bees. A pistol was produced
but not fired. All other unities were upheld.

I watched from the loft with my sister Scout,
an albino embryo in a jar. The Africans
assured us our father was the good man,
the one on veal rails, half frozen. My baby tooth
refused to fall out—resolved by string
and a bag of wooden bricks. The green shag rolled
on and on like the Sargasso Sea. *Your mind
and you.* "Ar, ar," said the pirates. "Lead us to booty!"
Pecans in the black soil, protective fuselage
made of the trees' canopy overhead. Mother
fixed a picnic, but inside the bread, I found
father's gold and lace crêpe teeth.

Illness

It's happened again. The bugaboo of illness, ingenuous little
death machine on my shoulders, in my spine and latissimus
dorsi muscles—no, deeper, fourth layer, spinalis dorsi, page 343
of *Gray's Anatomy*—and in the groin. I run on. I'm nowhere near dying,
but the fatigue runs through me all day like a poorly heated car
on an endless road through a Kansas winter, the draft numbing my hands
and feet. And then "weariness follows, and the infinite ache."
So I'm trying to abide with illness, feel it as the little
death it is, the link no one wants to speak of.
Parents never tell their children illness is death's half-sister,
and abiding with her, welcoming even, would be good practice.

A poem can be *A Little Instruction Manual for Things*:
"Death: A woman was dying and went to a teacher. 'My doctor
has given me only a few months to live. Can you help me?'
The teacher laughed. 'You see, we are all dying. It's only
a matter of time. Some of us sooner than others.'
Accepting death, the woman took a practice and was
healed, or died, it didn't matter then. . . . Plumbing: The pipe
should not come in contact with lime mortar or lime concrete
as the pipes can be affected by lime. When the pipes
are embedded in walls or floors, they should be covered
with Hessian cloth dipped in Coal Tar/Japan Black."
Or instructions for your own coup d'état. *Honey,*
where is that lovely terza rima on tile cutting?

But many poets, like parents, remain practical. Hot drinks,
rest, and vitamin C. A stanza or two in *The New Yorker*.
More reasonable, I see. Especially when there's no belief in an afterlife
or rebirth. But few claim that completely. If so, more
people would say, "Die, it's no big deal. Every *body* does it."
And few say this. So I'm practicing today, trying to be patient
with the pain and nausea, thinking of the suffering of others
and how I contribute to it with a lack of attendance to their pains
and illnesses, even absent when saying *goodbye, goodbye,*
and the anger with my sons at times. (Other vices—I shouldn't
bore the reader with the assorted sordid details.) This practice

seems easy when home alone in front of the TV, or in the study with my lonely, aching bones and the typewriter's skeletal keys.

But the onset of wellness effaces this me.

THE STREET DOG SPEAKS

The click of ten nails on the blacktop—
my cup of ivories, my roulette, my little
gun boats of luck, my dice. Thrown
into the street, I wander by scent
and scrim of instinct. You see me by the big
way of many fast cars. Dicey, my chances
of making the crossing. I'd need
a veritable Ra (not Set!) to guide me
across without a scratch. But my life as roadside dog
has nothing to move you to act.
I'm scenery—today, I move, but tomorrow
you will find me a very grave dog, "poor
dogsbody's body" on the side of the road
you mindlessly travel, and may too
die on someday if your luck runs as thin
as the layer of fat on my
desperate, luminous bones.

FEAR FACTOR

After the endless cable trellis of death
lined with yellow flags waving
like the garland of vomit
out of a mouth that had said, *No fear*;
after the actual beard of bees,
200,000 venomous barbs loaded
on little fighters, all nicknamed
"Stinger" by their mother, the queen;
after a snack at the entomologist's
café, where a sad, sagging species of a man
cried quietly in the corner as
another young body
wolfed down his prized Madagascar
Hissing Cockroaches; and after
the endless Plexiglas boxes
and mazes, all locked at one
point or another, all lowered, slowly,
at the speed of breath, into cold,
cold water lit for the cameras, it's time
for the fear factor to kick in.

A quiet bar on a sound stage. A set.
A set up. A father enters. The father
you've never met. You have to sit
on adjacent bar stools and talk about
what happened to him. What happened
to you. No alcohol is served. The set
is locked for an infinite duration. You must
find some resolution. His eyes are
black smoking guns, his mouth
a Scylla of words, his head a balloon.

Or an older sister who lost you in the woods
when you were young, before
you were kidnapped and raised,
violently but alive,
by bears and wolves. You must have
a proper tea with her, and one wasp will be
released into the room for every drop
spilt. You must ask her why

she spent so long at the mirror in the bathroom
before coming out to a sky as blue
as your eyes without you.

Or a girlfriend who left you because of
the distance, a boyfriend who left you
for his own cold, wet pain—the LSD
is FDA approved for the show's use,
and it kicks in as you both are hung by
your heels to honestly work things out
before you can be released. Never mind
the tiny gnawing mouths of rainforest ants.
Nothing compared to what spills out.

Or yourself, left in the warm dark
of your own skin, twisting like a flag
in the vomit-laden wind of thoughts,
with a rash and a concrete floor
to aid in the self-made
inquisition, the healthy bastinado,
the cat-o'-nine-tails' mental rise and fall
until you drop the illusion of yourself
and your pain, or the signal
that you quit: a white dimpled golf ball
marked "Titleist" that bounces like
what's left of you.

ABSTRACT AUBADE

To avoid saying,
begin, say, with the white
of her most tenderest parts—homogenized milk or
fish bones of the Eskimo. Skin
with the glyphs of welts,
the sting of hand or crop. Sting of jellyfish?
You piss on it to take it down. Said James Dean
pissed in front of a movie crew
to calm himself. Known he smashed
his helium Spyder into a Ford Tutor
disguised as late day.

Not a word of her!
A palm tree. Serrated shadow on bosom. Body
that shifts like sands. And warm.
Did I say mouth of dates? The whiteness

of a Wednesday, snow falling outside the Jefferson Room
and always Saturdays in December.
Fire. Um, horns. They lock—eyes. Like the Seine—
a wrist, another wrist, sapwood,

the Arc de Triumph, a knee! River water winds
through this woman who seldom
locks me in the kiosk—
a key, roulade, a sauce, albumen.

The light she has, that surrounds her,
is not artificial and arrives
both before and after me.

I say goodbye but still bask.
She has a resplendent albedo.

THAT BIG OLD BEAR HUNGRY AGAIN

I must work on doors today.

       The studio door worked off   its
             hinges   by family,   fighting dogs
       wanting love.

          The boys' door misaligned.

       My eldest asks about CPR, illustrated
on a pamphlet posted
          by the back door.

Gross, my youngest responds when I speak
         of inflating lungs, massaging hearts. But he admits
      he'd save his brother this way
          if necessary.

           I think of her and exchanging breath until
              the oxygen ran out. A contest, a kiss of life
till one gave up and inhaled the rich air outside
            the closed pulmonary circuit.

       My eldest asks me to blow up his Legos and mix the ashes
           with his if something were to happen to him—   don't
let them fall into his younger brother's hands.

         The acrid odor of burnt plastic after detonation.

       I laugh. Ask why it would matter.
Yeah, you'd be dead, the younger one says.
       I wish them long life and suggest we drop it.

           Dead Tristan, dead Tristan, the younger one sings.
Shut your fat mouth, Tristan responds.
          Enough! I command, as I feel the enormous door of mortality
            swinging over our heads, threatening to   knock us
     over,   over,   all the way over (bodhi svaha)

anytime, someday, but hopefully not this one
as the early summer air and light
                    are   so   fine.

ORACULAR

The other day, my youngest son in the carrier
on my back and my body warm with the rhythm
of filling, shovelful by shovelful, the third
wheelbarrow load that would go to the garden,
I thought of how some dubiously elected
world leaders would benefit from mucking stalls.
The sun was out for the first time in weeks,
a bright hydrogen-supported star burning
and roiling roughly ninety-two million miles
away, one astronomical unit, AU, the perfect
distance for such a golden thing
as opposed to just over one's head.
Curious the difference distance can make,
like Kokura was almost Nagasaki.

And the rains were over for the moment,
heavy rains only lightly tinged with random
radioactive particles, still buzzing around the atmosphere
from '45 and then the '50s and '60s
when everyone joined in. I love
the clarity of light in the fall out
under the open wheel of sky turning bluer
unto itself until it almost turns black. And shoveling,
composting, made me think of how G. Snyder's
"Four Changes" contains enough answers
to end all the current nonsense: fossil fuel-based
transportation, an economy that insists
on cancerous growth, "bread ever more of
stale rags," tongues for wealth and power
at all costs, even war. The new manure
is hottest, and it's best to mix it with
shovelfuls of sand and older broken-down
material. And I thought of how few
of the "Four Changes" I really live.

I'm like a grub worm in the dirt, essential
to the process but unable to change it much.
My role seems set—consume, fatten,
shit, die. And the outcome of such
blindness makes me think of the other

September 11th, the one in 1973
when Pinochet's troops took over Santiago
and marched all the socialists and communists
to the Estadio Nacional with US-financed
guns at their backs. I think it must have been
hard to hear the echoes of soccer fans' cheers
amid the howls of men and women with broken
hands, arms, and legs, and no confessions to give,
nothing to confess. And I doubt the CIA
had to give a lesson on the breaking of bones,
as natural to the human race as love.

After all, even composting is a violent cycle,
with maggots writhing in a discarded orange
like demons carousing in the brain. And I wonder
if our monuments of education,
entertainment, and infrastructure will be
used for torture someday when the empire
falls, as all great empires do. Sometimes,
I can almost see the bodies of our innocent civilians
chained to water pipes in malls, to railings
in stadiums. Maybe some haunting Chinese
or Arabic song, or Sousa march, will echo
off the concrete as the strong arm or blow torch
or kitchen knife comes closer. "I didn't do
anything!" the civilian may scream. That's
the point—what we are not doing now
will hang us later.

Mais priez Dieu que tous nous vueille absouldre.
I don't mean to be melodramatic or maudlin,
just practical. My hope is of the same cloth—
put your back or foot or finger to the manual
wheel of composting or pedaling or typing
and turn it like a prayer wheel until you feel
human again. Something will absolve you then,
and you will find rebirth in this physical sphere,
mirror of all we are blind to or faintly hear.

How We Go

From the outside to the inside
like a tongue lathing an ice cream
on a violent August day. Seventy-two
thousand subtle energy channels in the body,
but when the hand stops moving,
you're done. *Drip, drip, drip.* And when
the yab-yum of blood orange
and Devonshire cream at the heart goes
topsy-turvy, the little consciousness
escapes. Those going to a Pure Land
exit the crown of the head.
Those going to Hell go
out the ass. Same process
for animals with all their diverse
sufferings and hopes. Dreams of the flea and
flea-bitten. Buddha Shakyamuni
was a flea, a monkey, an ox, all of these
once. Where was my mind? Ah,

escape, as in that song that goes,
There is no life I know
to compare with pure imagination.
Yes, consciousness moves wherever it
desires, sticks to nothing, while
the Invisible Bees of Time gather
the Infinite Pollen of the Phenomenal.
But how exhausting, those travels,
and there are all those fireplaces
to sit by, swings to swing on,
dandelions to blow, even
Chinese to learn, and that takes
many lifetimes, so the little consciousness
desires a body again. Your father's body
if you're to be a woman,
your mother's if you're to be a man.

Subtle-body Buddhist physiology
slips neatly into Freud's black leather glove,
like the little consciousness nestles
down in the mother's womb

for an angry nap, caught now,
done wandering except for in
the ocean of itself, roiled by
waves of desire, hatred, and ignorance
that undulate nonstop
in the radiator of the brand-new
shiny embryo. Again.

NOTES ON THE POEMS

Much of the rhythm of "Why Dogs Ingest Anything While the Human Mouth Remains So Sentimental" is inspired by a recording of T. S. Eliot reading "Sweeney Agonistes." The two quotes at the end of first part are from *Magic and Mystery in Tibet* by Alexandra David-Néel. The quote at the start of the fourth part is attributed to the painter Francis Bacon, and this part retells the myth of Actaeon and Artemis.

The phrase "settling on me like an x-ray apron" in "My Secret Fantasy Life" is a reworking of an image from Anne Lamott's *Bird by Bird*.

The drawing that inspired "Bim Gets Breakfast in the Love Kitchen" can be seen in *A Practical Guide to Autism: What Every Parent, Family Member, and Teacher Needs to Know*.

The first three lines of the second part of "Seven-Part Note to Suicide" are from Woody Guthrie's "I'll Eat You, I'll Drink You." The Jack Kerouac extract in the fourth part comes from *On the Road*.

The final stanza of "Nomads with Samsonite" consciously echoes the final stanza of Elizabeth Bishop's "Questions of Travel."

"The Poet At Seventeen" was inspired by Arthur Rimbaud's "Les Poètes de sept ans" and Larry Levis's "The Poet at Seventeen."

The quotes in "Splash Zone" are from Ezra Pound's "Canto II."

Thanks to Tom Dvorske and Tiffany Armand Dvorske for some of the text in "Triweekly Cimarron River Report, May 17th to August 28th."

In "Scope," "There is no there there" is from Gertrude Stein's *Everybody's Autobiography*.

Note: We didn't burn them, we hanged them in "Hagiography" is T. S. Eliot's footnote to Ezra Pound's comment about William Carlos Williams in Pound's essay "Dr William's Position": "None of his immediate forebears burnt witches in Salem."

The quotes in "Survival" come from "Grizz," an article by Douglas H. Chadwick in a 2001 issue of *National Geographic*.

In "Crêpes Dentelles," "Your mind and you," and the preceding reference to the Sargasso Sea, are from Ezra Pound's "Portrait."

In "Illness," the quote in the first stanza is from Pablo Neruda's "Body of a Woman."

In "The Street Dog Speaks," "poor dogsbody's body" comes from James Joyce's *Ulysses*.

The penultimate stanza of "Abstract Aubade" reworks some lines from The Flaming Lips' song "What Is the Light?"

The quote in the second stanza of "Oracular" is from Ezra Pound's "Canto XLV." The quote at the start of the last stanza is from a ballade by François Villon and can be translated as "But pray God that he absolve us all."

TIMOTHY BRADFORD is the author of the introduction to *Sadhus* (Cuerpos Pintados, 2003), a photography book on the ascetics of South Asia. In 2005, he received the Koret Foundation's Young Writer on Jewish Themes Award for his novel-in-progress based on the history of the Vélodrome d'Hiver, and from 2007 to 2009, he was a guest researcher at the Institut d'Histoire du Temps Présent in Paris. His poetry has appeared in numerous journals including *42opus, Bombay Gin, CrossConnect, DIAGRAM, Drunken Boat, ecopoetics, H_NGM_N, Mudlark, No Tell Motel, Poems & Plays,* and *Upstairs at Duroc.* He currently teaches English at the University of Central Oklahoma and lives with his wife, two sons, and an ever-changing menagerie just outside of Oklahoma City.

Made in the USA
Charleston, SC
13 July 2011